WE'VE ALL SEEN HELENA

We've All Seen Helena

Copyright © 2019 by Lip Manegio.

ISBN: 978-1-7324986-3-1

All rights reserved. No portion of this book may be reproduced in any form without permission from the publisher, except as permitted by U.S. copyright law.

Cover design and layout by Dave Mahan.

Edited and formatted by Josh Savory, Kaleigh O'Keefe, Michael Malpiedi, and Liv Mammone.

total facts known about gerard way was written in a seminar led by Safia Elhillo at the winter 2017 Winter Tangerine onsite workshop & originally appeared in Freezeray Poetry.

conversation between gerard way and my dysphoria originally appeared in Flypaper Magazine.

GAME OVER BOOKS

Game Over Books
www.gameoverbooks.com

"I'm not dead, I only dress that way."
-Boy Division, My Chemical Romance

Table of Contents

6   summoning ritual for gerard way

7   total facts known about gerard way

8   gerard way dyes my hair

9   self portrait as gerard way

10   gerard way finds my fanfiction.net account

11   gerard way asks who i used to be, so i tell them by erasing one of my high school freshman year fanfictions until i dig myself out of them one more time

12   ode to the former abscess in gerard ways tooth

14   at a show in oakland in 2003, gerard way yells 'this song is about suicide' & then tells the audience they 'gotta dance it up right now'

15   gerard way holds me through the panic

16   gerard way asks me if there are others

17   ekphrasis of a youtube video i saw when i was in eighth grade showing gerard way & frank iero kissing on stage

18   gerard way pulls my binder over my head

19   gerard way asks me how i chose my name, so i tell them everything that came before

20   conversation between gerard way & my dysphoria

24   gerard way does my eyeliner

25   gerard way talks back

26   gerard way shows me the constellations

summoning ritual for gerard way

find a basement. an unfinished one if you can—the closer you get to the dirt, the better. these are old bones you're digging up, so keep your spades close to your chest.

burn incense of your grandmother's breath and place a needle on a Smith's record—it doesn't matter which one, as long as Morrissey sounds sad.
this is the easy part.

now, reach down your throat and pluck out a vocal chord.
place it in a circle carved
with a switchblade on the floor.

next, mix a white paint chip with a bit of bourbon.
wait for the dissolve. pour. let it seep.

write your attempt count on a slip of black paper
and place it under your tongue.
wait for the dissolve. spit. let it seep.

find a bone. powder it. sprinkle the dust around the border of the circle. whisper the name of what it once was. if you don't know, lie. if you can't lie, then you're not ready for this magic yet.

this is the hard part.

hide a shirt under your bed for 20 years. it must be stolen from your father's bottom drawer. take it out now. place it in the center
of the circle.

burn it.

total facts known about gerard way *after safia elhillo*

gerard way was born in either outer space or new jersey, no one is really sure which, but it is known that he will die somewhere in orion's belt. gerard way leaves behind a comet tail of black eyeliner and glitter in his wake wherever he goes. gerard way is nonbinary / gerard way would've been nonbinary if he was born two decades later and knew all of his options. gerard way has said he uses either he/him or they/them pronouns. everyone uses he/him pronouns for gerard way. gerard way and their careful androgyny acted as guidebook for all the mid-2000's genderqueer sad kids in black nail polish who were too passionate about warped tour. gerard way spent too long on the edges of supernovas to notice their own starlight. gerard way didn't play a show sober until the second album. they lived in their mother's belleview basement with amber preserved bats & replica swords & dozens of pill bottles. gerard way named their first daughter bandit. gerard way has probably stolen more than they gave, but who was keeping count anyway. they could swagger into an arena & become extraterrestrial for the night, something the queer kids in the crowd could almost touch, almost be, but not quite. gerard way continuously made out with guitarist frank iero on stage during the projekt revolution tour, the same tour where they met their wife. they later called it adrenaline, not attraction. gerard way has never publicly called themself queer. still, we dug ourselves out of them. still, we wrote them into our own story. don't you know how hard it is to find someone you might be able to trust? someone who looks like they could wear your name? call it a false god, call it idolatry, call it marginalia, call it desperation, call it what it is: an unidentifiable object flying above and us choosing to believe.

gerard way dyes my hair

& now we are painted the same color,
two fire heads looking
into a fingerprint smudged mirror, side
by side. they leave
the bathroom to grab another, unbloodied
towel & i am left to stretch
the strands between my fingertips—
i pull back
my hand & it is smeared
red. i look in
the reflection & my cheeks
are still round.

we are living in the danger days now.
the *keep the blades locked in a drawer* days.
the *make sure everyone eats because god i would do anything for bones like that* days.
the *holy shit please dye my hair because i haven't seen myself in days* days.

the mirror is leaking now.
my bangs look black still
even though i was trying
for crimson, and the not-blood
is still dripping
down my cheek. gerard
walks back in.

self portrait as gerard way

i paint myself red & no one
asks my face how it wants to be named—

i pull on a dangling tank top & a swipe
of eyeshadow & nothing
else & can still see myself:
fully formed & shining—

i mean, i am the right shape
to fit the inbetween
without ever being told
i am too curved flesh,
too unjagged—

now, i am all sharp
corner bones, dripping
black denim & glittering,
all howling abscessed teeth & soft
driftwood eyes—

what i mean is,
i am still not a *man*
but at least i don't have to prove
just how my body bends.

gerard way finds my fanfiction.net account

you know, the one i ran with my ex-girlfriend
you know, the one with the username *Frerard_Freakz*

they force out that obligatory discomfort
laugh before the question rolls off their tongue
& i'm left to figure out an explanation

> *listen, long distance love makes you do stupid things in the name of teenage hormones. listen, i forgot the password years ago, i'd take it down if i could. listen, you can't make yourself a god & then get upset when a scripture gets written around you. listen, i never found a love that could mould itself to my shape, so i'm sorry if i dug a new one out of your riverbed. listen, let me tell you a story: once, i was reading a one shot & started crying. i didn't know why until i realized whose skin i was trying to crawl into. listen, i spent years searching for new bodies to live in, you were just convenient & there & so many others had visited the orchard that i didn't see the harm in picking a fruit for myself -- how could i not be disappointed when i got crabapple. i mean, the orchard was filled with trees with deep voices and perfectly flat chests. i mean, i still read fanfiction. i mean, i still try to cut myself out of this body and graft onto something else. i mean, i still haven't found a love that looks like me.*

gerard way asks who i used to be, so i tell them by erasing one of my high school freshman year fanfictions until i dig myself out of them one more time

                      my   bedroom was
             a half full
                                    throat,   stale
                                                          ceiling
growing   hazy thoughts.

  seemed   I was spending more and more time like this, living in
                                                                  eternity,
world without   clouds.   Nothing   could take away the

          bottled fire,   my burning mind.

Maybe it wasn't healthy, my dependence on

                        the weight   I woke
up   covered in,   a pounding in my head. And sure,
                       I almost lost
                me   .

I just
                   forgot   I was   love and anger and
every other   emotion besides   so   I wound up a
pile   in   the
stomach   of a bad thing.

ode to the former abscess in gerard ways tooth

> *the day my chemical romance was to record the song 'vampires will never hurt you,' gerard had just gone to the dentist for a rotting mouth and was fucked on painkillers. before going into the recording booth, the owner of his then-label punched him in the face & said "now go sing". he then gave what he considers to be the best vocal performance of his life.*
>
> *in an interview with noisey years later, producer geoff rickly said he took gerard's vicodin away because "he was singing a little lazy when he wasn't in pain"*

gerard wails *please save my soul*
& you know that moment where you can hear
a black eye through stereo speakers
they would say it was the worst pain they've ever been in

when i was two years old,
my molar betrayed me & was removed without novocaine
a different dentist later told us it could've been salvaged
& 17 years on, gerard is still breathing / soul sitting safely
under their tongue

now, there are no scalpels in sight / except the ones we hold ourselves

when a man in a nonfiction workshop asks me to talk about the [   ]
he is saying *you are writing a little lazy when you're not in pain*
& the blisteringly bright danger days charts six spots below the
martyrdom of the black parade

i mean, everyone loves the abscess, the hollow
they can curl themselves into, everything just
decay enough to tear out and not make them gag on the stench

but there is a video where gerard gapes his mouth
into a smile and you can see the filling shining,
showing where the ache has scabbed over

listen, all i'm saying is:
there is more to a body / than its wounded howling

think of all the things we could save
if we just gave them time to heal
instead of bringing out the knives

at a show in oakland in 2003, gerard way yells 'this song is about suicide' & then tells the audience they 'gotta dance it up right now'

the song was *headfirst for halos*
a bright guitar riff under a plea of
                            i think i'll blow my brains against the ceiling
& gerard always said he brought the bullets,
never promised not to use them
just made his hurt as danceable as he could

they were drunk, stumbling across the stage
cracking themself open for a crowd that barely knew their name
their voice broke so many times it was like an audible fracture
at one point he was bowing into the audience
howling *you don't know, you don't know*
& i wonder how many times they went on a stage
expecting to never walk off it,
how many times he performed his own burial,
showed us just what a coffin could look like
we've all seen helena,
we all know how beautiful a death can look
if everyone plays their parts right

& yeah, i've done it too,
thrashed my pain into a song until i could show someone else
& have them call it art
bent my sickness into something you could move to
what are either of us but depressed bastards
screaming about how *rock n' roll will save your life*
what are we if not dancing along to our own funerals

gerard way holds me through the panic

they are used to it now / don't pretend
to understand anymore / but doesn't mind
when i ask them to sing that song again
about being unafraid
or the one about being so afraid
you can't even sleep
                doesn't mind when i scrape myself
                off the roof of his mouth
he asks me to describe
the fear & all i can say is
                it's not like tremors, it's worse than tremors,
                there are these terrors
& there i go again,
telling my story through someone else's
tongue / its just that
when i get like *this*
it can be hard to feel my own teeth
gerard forgives, of course,
the way i gum out their own confession
back to them / hand him back
all his old knives

gerard way asks me if there are others

i was a twelve-year-old sad b*y when i clicked on a music video thumbnail
& *boom*—there he was—the short, italian guitarist
in all his twenty-somethings glory
screaming into a microphone, guitar hung in a vice grip around his neck
being everything i could have if only
everything had been different
i didn't know i was [   ] yet / just how hard i wished
to lay my fingers on frets in the same shape as him

the first time i saw frank iero live was in a cramped basement venue
my chemical romance had dissolved until there was nothing left
but the cellabration
& here he was, singing like he was dying
so close i could see the way his chest rose and fell
in the way i dreamt of imitating

when my stepfather asked if frank was my *heartthrob*
i said yes, because i didn't know what else to call this
infatuation, maybe? / threat of desire pumping through my veins, maybe?
envy, deadly sin, maybe? / i guess you could call it sin to want
to see myself reflected / back in photographs
as sweat soaked bare chested tattoo layered god under
arena lights / call it wanting
to make myself into false idol / into something
that could sheen beneath the shine
and not just melt / under all that heat

ekphrasis of a youtube video i saw when i was in eighth grade showing gerard way & frank iero kissing on stage

there it is | my boyhood | on a jumbotron | a queerness | i didn't yet know i had | framed in a 16:9 aspect ratio | frank's arms wrap around gerard | & both of their hair is too long | to see their mouths | it is so easy to pretend to be | a faceless thing | *you know what they do to guys like us* | & god, i wish i did | gerard breaks away to go hymn across the stage | hips jutting like daggers | as they strut in whatever | direction they choose | & frank returns to the thrash | like he is writhing out his own body | i try to find myself somewhere | in the ragged space | left on the expanse of stage | but there is only so much | that can be fit into a thirty second clip | & there just isn't room for me | trying to slice my way | between two bodies | that were never mine to want

gerard way pulls my binder over my head

i called them in here after my arm got caught
on the upswing
& now it seems we are both waiting
for the wane,
for the strangle to become too much
i tell him i wore the creature
for nine hours straight today
& they just sigh—expected
he can tell i'm cracking now,
offers me a rib of his own
& knows all i want is subtraction
they have seen how i green eye
the way his shirt falls,
has watched the gentle simmer for years,
& now look
all artificial boy with artificial nothing
gathering themself in front of their reflection
gerard mentions the way my skin pulls back
& i say nothing
of how i dream to recede into their skeleton
gerard sees the rattle
& says nothing
of a dress wishing to be filled
just keeps stripping
back the way i've painted myself
into a knife

gerard way asks me how i chose my name, so i tell them everything that came before

(i never told you what i do for a living redux)

i keep a book of the names / i have given / *the bodies i claim* / with my want / everytime my chest / heaves itself away / from a skeleton / *touched by angels* / but / *falling from grace* / i mean / i had to invent a new language / just to perch on the tip of someone's tongue / *never again / and never again* / already been buried too many times / *i'm so dirty, babe* / so mouthed over and spit back out / have you ever seen something so dripping / *a stain that never comes off the sheets* / have you ever seen something / so splayed open / as a name / asking to be rewritten / *stay out of* / *the prayer* / *and i'll grieve*

conversation between gerard way & my dysphoria

*(in which the part of
gerard way is played
by erasures of his
own lyrics)*

I never thought it'd be
      you
                asking for
A thousand bodies

                          i only ever asked for one body
                          one that lets me breathe right
                          and i guess i'll chase it if i have
                          to

You're running after

      fire

                          & you do know a fire can't
                          burn without fuel, right?

No I mean
      you can't burn inside

                          & i've been twisting ember
                          since i started sprouting &
                          became a shape that couldn't
                          imitate you anymore, you walk
                          around in all that effortless
                          androgyny how could you not
                          think that you were feeding
                          something

If
      you light

         my   *gown*

                                        don't pretend the smolder is a
                                    threat, how could you even know this
                                            heat through all that skin

    I'm
                    the mess you made,

  the best damn dress

    you   *fear.*
you
     are young

                your hopeless hair

     never wanted   *to be this way*
                                            have you heard yourself lately
                                            you sound just like my mother
                                            bringing up my age do you
                                            want to see all the hair shed
                                            into bathroom sinks the dye
                                            spent on this shock do you
                                            know how much i've bled do
                                            you want me to show you this
                                            body's hips do you want to see
                                            the scars do you know

Well,

You should've
       been a better son,
             the infection
They can amputate at once.
You should've been

                                                      tell me again all the things i
                                              should have been how i have
                                            torn things so far apart and
                                       then tell me how i should've
                            been *better* what do you know

I think you

       pretend

                     you're

breathing,
  I think

           we all shake,

I think

It's liveable,

I'm kind of miserable, too—

                                                 i get it you think you
                                      understand this rot but you
                                      move with all that swagger in
                                    your hips in a bulletproof vest
                                  how could you hurt what proof
                                                  do you have

You got blood
               in your eye.
I mean

    the world don't need
Another hopeless cause -

                                                                          too late the drip already started
don't you know i try to find you
in every reflection do you know
how many mirrors i've blotted
myself out of

I'll give you

gasoline,
    would you

        make a saint of

            burning

                              would you make a martyr of
the way i die in so many
people's mouths listen i wish i
could stop the scorch but what
do you want me to do

Trust
        the words in your head

           please understand it has to be this way

gerard way does my eyeliner

they carve it on
with such soft hands
you would think them a brush
& me stretched canvas
laughs as they say
is this what you always wanted
to be painted in this image
& i pull down my waterline
show them every secret
i have ever kept
they huff another chuckle
say something about dramatics
as they drag the black
draw a curve sharp enough
to keep me safe

gerard way talks back

what i'm going through, shot lip gloss through my veins

   & you still are wondering what   is inside of me
   listen, there is only so much you can ask of me   only so much
      story you can write in someone else's chest
   i know what you think i'm made of   but you're wrong
          i'm not that kind of girl   too bound up
   in bulletproof vests & chipped nails   to save anyone else
     do you know how much   i hide in my waterline
   do you know   what i keep under the bed
     we've all got skeletons   how could you ever think
   you had touched mine   do you even know
            how a broken bone snaps
   you're right   about one thing though
   i was never gash enough   there were never enough
   rips to find my way home through   but yeah,
   i sure looked pretty walking down the street   listen, this isn't
   what everyone thinks it is   desperate grab at teenage rebellion
            man clinging to his youth
     you saw the way i can make dirt fly
       did you think a man   could do that
   did you think   anything that wasn't dying
            could do this

it's not a fashion statement, it's a fucking deathwish

gerard way shows me the constellations

look — that's where i was born — look — that's where we're all heading to — look — those stars are still yours to name — look — look how bright they burn — how far the light has traveled to reach us — how far a star can fall — there is so much up there dying — but not us — not now — listen to me — orion is not a tombstone — and neither are you — there is so much light behind your eyes — so much unspent — your body was not meant to incinerate — look — there's a shooting star — look — i can see your reflection in it — look — comets don't come around often, kid — you gotta love them while you can

Acknowledgements

All of the thanks in the world to Gerard Way for shining so bright and showing me everything I ever wanted to be. I hope he doesn't think this whole thing is creepy.

Myles Taylor for being my ride or die, the only person that can put up with my Virgo sun/Aquarius moon ass consistently. For being the person to lovingly shove me into this whole 'poetry thing' in the first place. I would be nowhere close to where I am without you.

The Emerson Poetry Project & The Cantab Lounge for being the walls that first bounced these words back to me.

Bradley Trumpfheller for all of the edits & the turtlenecks. Sara Mae for showing me just what words can do. Brandon Melendez for teaching me the word 'stoge' & so much else. Truj for the tender church that was Penrose Diner breakfasts & for always so intentionally holding space. Kayla LaRosa for the trips to Wendy's & the gut busting laughs. De Etienne for being the least reliable Aquarius in the world, but still pulling it together when it counts. Every other member of the NorthBeast community who has ever made room for me, there are too many to mention but I love y'all so very much.

Chloe & AJ & Briana for getting me through high school. Alex Estrada & Lauren Lopez for getting me through the summer. Elle Watson for bringing K-Pop & a heck of a lot of light into my life. Mika Earley for somehow agreeing to split a room with me for two years, while not killing me. Adrienne Novy for being the kindest & gentlest cheerleader throughout this whole project, and the first eyes many of these poems ever met.

Everyone at Game Over Books for putting so much work into getting this weird, strange book off the ground and into your hands.

My mother for putting up with all my teenage, emo phase angst in the moment. My grandmother for being the toughest person I have ever met (in the best way). Luke for being someone to grow up with. Jack for being someone who made growing up worth it.

Lip Manegio is a trans, queer nonbinary poet based in Boston where they are working towards a BFA in creative writing at Emerson College. Their favorite pastimes include smiling at dogs they pass on the street and crying to My Chemical Romance on public transit. They represented Emerson at CUPSI 2018 in Philadelphia, appeared on finals stages at FEMS 2018 and Capturing Fire International Queer Poetry Slam & Summit 2018, and were a member of the winning team at the 2018 Vox Pop Poetry Tournament. Their work has appeared in or is forthcoming from Flypaper Magazine, Crab Fat Magazine, the minnesota review, Tin House, and elsewhere.